THE STORM WITHIN

SAYALI WAGLE

Made with ♥ on the Notion Press Platform
www.notionpress.com

Almost 3 years after Horizon, I looked at the sea that tries to reach it. As I faced the good and bad in life, some good souls set an example of what living looks like. We all might or might not be on the same boat, but we're definitely surfing through the same waters. The calmness of the sea is a blessing and the storms are inevitable. In the struggle to stay afloat, we miss out on a lot of beauty. I would love to dedicate this book to both - the calm and the storm, and the good souls that journeyed along and became guides as we sailed to different shores. I hope we enjoy the journey as we try to get to know the sea better every day. This one is for the wonderful people I've met on the way who've left a piece of their heart with me. Thank you for becoming the light. I promise to sail with love.

Contents

Preface   *vii*

1. CALM AMIDST CHAOS   1

2. THE LIMITLESS CREATION   3

3. THE STORM WITHIN   5

4. ENIGMA   7

5. MORNING   9

6. WITNESS OF DEATHS   10

7. PRICED   12

8. ANCHORED   13

9. NOON   15

10. IN THE MIDDLE OF NOWHERE   17

11. LESSONS FROM THE SEA   19

12. MOONRISE   20

13. TWILIGHT   21

14. NEARER TO THE STARS   23

15. MIDNIGHT   25

16. HOME   27

17. THE STORM BEFORE THE CALM   28

18. THE CARRIER OF LIFE & DEATH   30

19. TO THE RESCUE   32

20. A NEW WORLD   34

PREFACE

When I was a kid, I had been to a few coastal regions. I have been there numerous times after that. One thing that fascinated me as a kid was what a fisherman told us about a boat tied to an anchor with pretty garlands. He said that a new boat or ship, before setting out in the waters, is married to the sea. It is a ceremony where the rituals are carried out like any other wedding and only then, the ship (the bride) is sent to the sea (the groom). In this book I have tried to personify the ship and the sea. To imagine how the ship's life at sea could be. The book ahead, is the ship talking to you!

I

CALM AMIDST CHAOS

I stand by the shore, waiting to be fully occupied. A weight, a number, a limit that is considered as the ideal burden that I can take.

A lesser number means that I don't have enough to carry. Lesser feet on my being, mean that it is less than what I can and should tolerate; it means that it is too easy for me; that my existence isn't being fully utilized.

I know I have to leave the shore for the destination unknown to me. Home is new everyday. Everyday, the route is the same, yet I feel I do not know the sea.

I had cursed the sea at times, for his anger made me fear for my life. I could see the world that the sailor chose to show me. I believed the world I saw through his eyes while the sea screamed to tell me that he wasn't the one to be blamed. But, I cursed the sea for being rough. All he had done was scream to let me free.

So many feet have started wandering around. I can sense them all. The happy jumping, the tired walk, the regret of leaving, the eagerness for the destination; all of them with either a purpose to fulfill or the grief of a lost purpose.

Some heading back home, some moving away from it. Some willingly, some with eyes fixated on the shore. I carry the weight of a hundred emotions, a thousand regrets, and a million dreams. Could anyone put a limit on that?

I am calm today. It has been years I've been at sea. Years with the same sailor. I do not know how many trips it ideally takes for a ship to learn to be calm amidst the chaos. But today I am calmer than ever.

II

THE LIMITLESS CREATION

There are so many footsteps. Everyone is rushing to their spaces to settle, excited to explore the waters. They might have heard from people about the beauty of the sea.

They're probably aware that the sea is unpredictable. But they've believed him.

They have faith that he will be calm till they reach, that he will be hospitable till he hands them over to the land.

Some have left reluctantly while some look forward to the destination. Very few are looking forward to the journey.

Very few are welcoming the sea with open arms, for they do not ask of him to be a certain way, for they know that they are tiny beings at his mercy.

They pray to him to be gentle to me; for their life depends on how the sea treats me. Most of them unpack and adore the stay and food.

I pity them; those who fear the vastness of the sea that is meant to be adored. How little of life they must have experienced to adore the ship when the sea, the true creation, is singing a melodious song?!

How little life they must know to prefer to stay within the walls and peek into the world outside, than to step out in the open and peek within?

III

THE STORM WITHIN

There is a lot of chatter within. Something that I cannot avoid.

The strangers are talking to each other, getting to know their stories, wanting to let time pass. They judge each other based on the stories they've been told in a few hours.

And here, despite hearing numerous stories from the waters over the years, I do not fully know the sea.

But none of these people care. Neither the one who judges, nor the one being judged. They are just passing their time in the long journey. A few want to be with themselves, a few are observing the sea, writing verses about him which would forever be hidden or dropped in the waters for him to read.

The noise grows louder and I feel dizzy. I realize, like every other day, that the storm within is not mine, but of the others trying to pass their precious time. I cannot help it. Instead, I listen to the sea until the noise starts to fade.

IV
ENIGMA

I am leaving for the journey. I usually cherish the few hours of comfort before I am loaded. But not once did I get a few seconds away from the sea. We both wouldn't mind a few breaths without each other.

I envy the sea at times; many times, I must say. I'm nothing without him, but he is whole, he probably holds another world within. He is whole without me, without anything you can think of.

I wish to ask him someday. What does it feel like? To have a world depend on you but to have none to depend upon?

I envy him for how he is worshipped by every being. But I'm sure I'll pity him if I know him more than the waves; more than what he tells me he is.

I leave, knowing that I'll be here again.

I look at the anchor being let loose, taking a breath before he has to stop another of my mates from wandering into the sea.

I set out, unsure of my return.

When you have the vastness and depth of the sea, you do not hope for a smooth journey, but, instead, for strength to face the waves.

V
MORNING

We have left the shore with the Sun shining bright. I see him every morning and wonder whether my life will be like his; a neverending routine of showing up irrespective of my will.

Of course, my end is evident unlike his. How difficult it must be to be the one every being needs but hates to be! No one would want to keep burning to be the light.

I wish I could let you rest for a day by being the fire. Just a day, because I don't want to be you. Because the light is never appreciated until it starts getting darker.

The sea is reflecting the Sun's light. Ironic, how the sea can kill any fire but a distance between them gives the most beautiful and mesmerizing view. I sail through it, through the shiny waters!

VI
WITNESS OF DEATHS

I look at the swaying trees, the wind brushing through their being.

From a distance as far as ours, I feel like they're waving me goodbye as I pass by them. I wonder if the ones closer to the sea talk to him.

I have seen the sea carry leaves and branches at times. So I know that he knows them. The sea carries their dead bits and broken pieces. Do they think that he wants to remind them of what they have lost? I hope they don't.

I hope they know how difficult it is to carry death, forever.

The ones who have survived their loss think that they're being reminded of it. But the sea carries the remains home; the remains reside within him.

But the sea is still strong as ever. He keeps the remains close enough to feel the losses yet doesn't let them reach the depths of his soul; for the depths of his soul are meant for the existence of life.

The deaths that reach the bottom of the soul are fed to the life within; not cherished and taken care of.

VII
PRICED

The place we are heading is my home; where I was built.

I knew that there was no going back once I'm sent to the sea. Only when the sea has worn me enough to show my age, I could go back to land.

The hands making me never got to take me to the sea. The hands taking me through the sea will never know my birth.

I wonder what went into the making; to make someone so strong that they take ample load yet keep going, all while staying afloat. Because much would be lost if I drown; much that I hold within.

Is that all that matters? What goes with me?

I feel I'm just priced, not valued.

What if I take a plunge into the sea when there isn't a single person or thing onboard? Will I be searched for? Or will a new ship start taking birth, to be married to the sea, to be forgotten if she took a plunge alone?

VIII
ANCHORED

The Captain is sailing with me for the thousandth time, maybe. He is young but has gotten tired really soon.

I was looking forward to challenging the waves together but looks like he'll give up any time now. I think it is just a matter of time before he starts thinking of home; the four walls of comfort.

The Sea hears it. The Sea hates it; the thought of comfort, the feel of comfort.

The Captain is not what he was the first time we had sailed. I don't think he remembers that this is his milestone trip.

We both get to rest at the destination. But he gets to explore new lands while I get some alone time with the sea.

The anchor, I think, wishes to let go at times. But not always because he is tired of holding on to someone who'll eventually be freed, but because, even when I'm left alone, even if I wish to, he sees that I cannot venture out to explore.

Of course, I'd be lost. But that is the thing.

I know that the sea is vast enough to hold me close, abundant enough that I wouldn't feel the need to go searching for the shore.

The Captain, mindfully exploring the land, lost in the chaos of the world, wouldn't know what it is like to be lost in a love as pure as the sea.

Is that why I'm tied to the anchor as he roams the streets freely?

Because humans think drowning in the abundance of love is riskier than drowning in the noise of this chaotic world?

IX

NOON

The sun is the brightest today. But, well, I feel this everyday.

The curtains are closed. No one even tries to peep out. The brighter he shines the lonlier he gets. That has never dissuaded him from shining the brightest.

So what has been said is true; very few can see you shine.

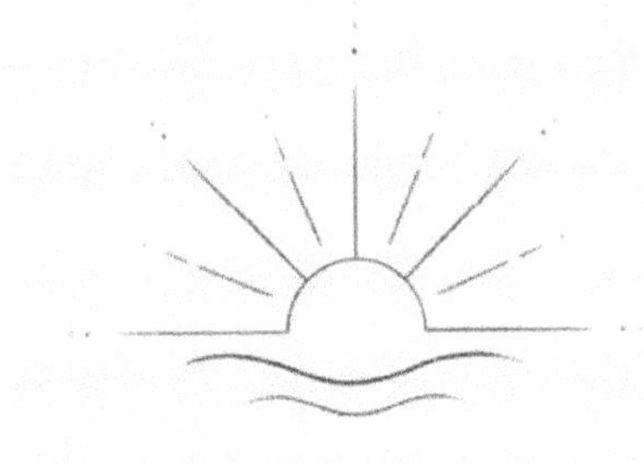

It's a lazy afternoon after a heavy meal. The Captain has cursed the Sun several times by now. I think he grows stronger every time someone curses him for being too bright for them to see.

But he understands that he cannot be loved throughout the day, in any form, any behaviour. He knows that not all of them have drawn the curtains to stay away from him.

There are some who let him be, who have chosen to stay in, who will wait patiently for him to become calmer when they cannot help him in his brightest yet lowest.

He RISES for them; he SETS for them!

IN THE MIDDLE OF NOWHERE

We've reached a place from where no land or city-like views are visible. It is all nature around us for as far as the eye can see.

The waters, the trees, bright sky, and the horizon. I wonder what lies beyond it.

The horizon that we see as a thin line dividing the two worlds, is actually an unending confluence.

You will end up travelling the world waiting for them to part ways but that is the beauty of the horizon. It divides the two worlds with so much grace and delicacy that they keep meeting endlessly despite their individual vastness.

At this point, the human tires; of the nature, of lack of man-made views.

They do not realize the happiness within. They try to keep finding new things, forgetting that there is variety in the seemingly monotonous nature around, only if you are keen enough to look.

They say to each other when they cannot see a single man-made view around, "We're in the middle of nowhere." But look around, my dearest, you're in the middle of God's creation and there's nothing within sight that can make you feel anything but blessed.

Take it in until you spot the land; until you go back to the places where you start to crave nature and finally, actually, sit in the middle of nowhere.

XI

LESSONS FROM THE SEA

The sailor often reminisces about the initial days. Sometimes I fear whether he is alert at sea.

That is the thing about memories, good or bad; once you test the waters with your feet, you find it warm; warm enough to get you to walk in. And before you know it, you're drowning.

He is doing the same today. His mind is not at sea. He loved the sea while on land. I remember how he loved the time he spent alone at sea, how the sea let him see his reflection, and how, as he kept looking, he saw life in the depths of his soul.

The sea taught him to be vast, as vast as you can, to hold beauty within; the beauty so mesmerising that only the brave will dare to dive in, only the passionate will stay a bit longer to witness the magic, and only the empaths will add a tear to his vastness as they see the wrecks that he holds within.

XII

MOONRISE

The early evenings are wonderful and energetic. The rough waves feel adventurous. The chatter feels like light music. The skies co-operate.

I can see both, the Sun and the Moon, residing in the blue skies; together. They face each other, as if to confront each other. To ask for their dues.

The Sun wanting to know why he does not get to witness the calm, the Moon wanting to know why he gets to witness the tears instead of the hustle.

They envy each other for a moment before they realize that they're seeing each other from a distance so far, a whole world exists in between! A world that depends entirely upon them.

They realize that they both have to be the givers and neither has it easy; that one has to be the listener as he seeks one, while the other has to shine so bright that his own light masks his sorrows.

They both exchange a glance before they understand the other; before the Sun steps down to let the Moon rise.

XIII
TWILIGHT

It's twilight.

Moments before I have to squint my eyes to look around.

I feel the most during this time. I understand the most now. There is something that happens within when you are with nature around twilight.

You think. You are made to think.

Even now, everyone is watching the sea, taking lessons from him. They look at the setting sun as if asking him to wait a little longer, wanting to absorb every ounce of beauty when they can.

I think they are trying to take in the calm to balance the chaos within.

The sun won't wait. I know. We've complained enough when he was here. You cannot ask him to stay only through his beautiful phases. He does not stay at one's convenience. You cannot ask him to stay just enough for the light and warmth and curse him for the scorching heat.

Everyone is in deep thought. I can sense the calm.

They wish for this time to stop to reflect, to have a deep conversation with oneself.

The sun is about to leave. But not without pinpointing one's pain; not without reminding them of their painful past they've been avoiding for the longest time.

I have never sensed happiness at this time of the hour. It is a time to reflect. Before the ball of fire takes a night-long dip into the sea to emerge again knowing that he might not be wanted, but that he's needed, everyone is alone, till the moon takes over.

So many people sit alongside each other, yet everyone has to be alone for a while; after the sun leaves and before the moon arrives.

XIV

NEARER TO THE STARS

I see a plane passing as I sway to the music of the sea. It is louder and harsher but I'm swaying anyway.

I look at the plane, fighting the air as I fight the waters so as to not get lost.

I wonder if he can see the moon and stars nearer and clearer than I can. I wonder if he gets to experience the journey like I do. I wonder if he'd like to.

I would like to be amongst the clouds for a day. I'd ask them if they talk to the stars.

I'd tell them how the sea brings them closer to me and how I think they can hear me despite the distance.

I'd tell them how the sea is made up of their tears; that I sail through their grief daily and I know everything without its depths.

"I'm made up of just tears", the cloud thinks. I'd tell him that he probably qualifies as a living being, for they are alive as long as there are tears.

I don't know how the plane will survive the rough waves. It wouldn't be the same as air.

Would he like the sea better than the winds? Would he have the patience to just be with the sea? To understand him? To sway to the music of the sea yet not get lost in it?

It's better to serve our purpose, my friend.

For I am meant to know the grief of the clouds but not watch them weep. For the plane, who knows their sorrows but cannot dive into it despite being co-travellers, would never understand the sea.

XV
MIDNIGHT

It is midnight. I can't see the way ahead.

All has been left to God. All is left to the sailor. My life is now in their hands.

I can't see but only feel and hear. I hear the sea at night more than any other time. Sometimes, I feel, one relies much more on the sight than on the sound. That is how the words are missed and misread.

I can now feel what "going with the flow" means. Of course, there is someone to show me the way. But I have no choice but to blindly trust him.

I am just floating in water. I can see the moon and stars. Maybe they know where I'm heading.

Sometimes I see them in water. I'm grateful to the sea for bringing us closer. Whenever I'm at the harbor, I talk to them. I tell them I wish to feel the sky. They tell me they wish to feel the sea.

We just smile knowing we can't; knowing we don't have to.

XVI
HOME

The Sailor seems tired; more than any other day in all this time that I have spent with him at sea.

For the first time, he is thinking of his last day at sea. I wonder what made him feel this.

Our first day at sea was also our first day together. So, I know him as much as I know the sea. Maybe a little less. I stay with the sea when he goes home.

He is terribly missing home today. He started full of enthusiasm. He has never missed home so much before.

I think it is time for us to part ways. We both are getting old.

He has been at sea for as long as I remember. He has started cursing the sea recently. He used to love the waves. He used to love swaying with them.

He is thinking of home. He remembers his wife and kids, and how he barely knows his family.

He is thinking of parting with the sea. He is tired of swaying. For the first time, he thinks of his farewell with the other sailors.

He wishes it is on land. He wishes for his feet to be stable.

XVII

THE STORM BEFORE THE CALM

He made a mistake. He chose the sea and while at it, thought of stability. What a fool!

Does he not know that it is sin to wish for a cool breeze when you've chosen fire? Does he not know that the sea can hear him wish for stability?

The sea rumbles; growls and roars you may say.

Suddenly, I feel a commotion inside me. The feet sound different. I have never felt this uneasy. I do not know this feeling. Why is everyone running?

I can also feel the sailor shiver. I don't spot anything.

The Sun is letting me know about his arrival. He is making sure I cannot see what beholds. Now I can just hear and feel.

I feel lighter than usual. I feel the sea's anger. But it's not for me.

I failed to realize the love. I failed to see that his fight was not with me, but for me; to free me. There's too much hustle; inside and around me.

I think I'm sinking! Is it the storm before the calm?

XVIII

THE CARRIER OF LIFE & DEATH

I am feeling lighter with time. The commotion inside and around me is fading.

I feel like I'm looking at the sea differently now. I have started to get to know him. I can see his soul; probably the reason behind his uncertainty, instability.

He holds so much within; so much, that the growls were like a mere shedding of tears while you're...well, there's no analogy to his suffering. Probably, someone on land might use the sea's pain to describe theirs. That is how much he has endured.

He is so much more than what I have seen in my lifetime.

He carries life and death, things and flesh, calm and chaos; all at a time, residing within.

I see some light. The Sun is co-operating now. I can see everything that the sea had been meaning to tell me all this time. I feel so calm.

I don't know where I am but here, nothing matters, there's silence, there's stillness.

Yes, there's stillness within the sea. I don't feel my life but I feel his.

I rest peacefully while the land is full of chaos, screams, cries, and mainly, feelings and emotions; something that the sea has taken away from me. Maybe that is why I felt lighter. That is why I stopped feeling much.

I have hit rock bottom.

XIX

TO THE RESCUE

There are many people struggling to get to me. Or maybe I feel like they are. But, no!

You know how it feels when you have been the savior all this while, carrying the burden of hundreds of lives and when you are sinking, there's a silent commotion around you? A silent commotion inside you?

One of these people around me must have felt this sometime. Maybe they pity me now.

There's silence. There's a deep silence within. I can't name it.

I was okay without a reward all these years. I didn't expect one by the end. But, at this point, I think I wished for a smile, a nod that could reassure me that my existence is known, seen, acknowledged.

I know there's no point feeling bad when things have ended. Who am I to decide who deserves the most care, whose end is most tragic, who has endured the most!

Maybe they were carriers too, all these people. But unlike me, they didn't get a chance to unload before they were loaded with a new set of burdens. Maybe they deserve more.

Whatever is going on around me looks like a rescue operation. I see many people trying to find the remains.

I am just a piece of trash that is making their work difficult. But I can't move. I really want to.

I have very little strength left. The strength that I was admired for on the surface. But here, I can be calm. Here, I have another life to begin; the one that I wouldn't get to live otherwise.

I just shut my eyes and wait for everyone to leave - the living and the dead.

Once they leave, I'll rest with the sea; within the sea.

XX

A NEW WORLD

Every person is brought back to land; their destination.

Hundreds of emotions, thousands of regrets, and millions of dreams lay still; maybe, glad that they were finally on the surface after being suppressed for ages.

Despite knowing there were no survivors, despite knowing there is no life in those dreams, someone took the effort to reach rock bottom to let them on the surface. I wish someone had taken these efforts while there was still hope, while there was still breath, while the dreams were full of life.

The Sailor, unknowingly, sailed for the last time and rested for the first.

The sea knows all the stories. Now, the land will, too.

I live in the sea and the sea, finally, is calm. The calmness after a lifelong struggle. The calmness that is relieving but also makes you question, "Now what?"

The struggle ended but the calmness was unsatisfying. Because you've never known what it felt like.

What do you do then? When a lifetime is spent on one purpose, and it ends with a fullstop?

You feel dead inside. But you are meant to live more, feel more just when you think this is what rock bottom feels like. And like a dead survivor, you have to pick your broken self and head back home to find a new purpose, a beauty you do not know unless you dive in; something you never thought existed all this time.

Who knew there was so much life, abundance, and calm until I drowned?!

Who knew drowning just meant finding a world you knew nothing of?!

Write to me at: write.sayali@gmail.com

* 9 7 9 8 8 9 7 7 7 4 8 2 1 *

She does not await the shore. She knows that her life is in the sea. How long could one fear the storms?
"Do not find peace in the storms," she says. Be the peace that is undeterred by the storm.
979-889777482-1
9 798897 774821

POWERING
SUCCESS
SHAPING
LEADERS
-THE-
MENTOR
-ADVANTAGE-
RICHA SINGH